Silly Aunt Tilly

written by Jennifer Jacobson
illustrated by Tuko Fujisaki

HARCOURT BRACE & COMPANY

Orlando Atlanta Austin Boston San Francisco Chicago Dallas New York
Toronto London

My Aunt Tilly went to
the North Pole one day.
She left me behind,
I am sad to say.

Aunt Tilly came home with birds in her hair. And she brought something back for me.

My Aunt Tilly went to
the rain forest one day.
She left me behind,
I am sad to say.

Aunt Tilly came home with bees in her hair. And she brought something back for me.

My Aunt Tilly went to the city one day. She left me behind, I am sad to say.

She shared a ride with a big, green fish.

Aunt Tilly came home with a crown in her hair. And she brought something back for me.